# Tree Life

by Kara Black

# What You Already Know

Different parts of a plant work together to help it live and grow. The parts of a plant's leaf system make food for the plant. The plant's root system brings water and minerals up to the stems. The plant's stem system carries water and minerals to leaves and other parts of the plant. It also supports the plant.

Plants and trees can be grouped by their roots, stems, and leaves. Coniferous trees grow seeds in cones. Deciduous trees lose their leaves in the fall.

Plants reproduce in different ways. Most plants make seeds, which can form in flowers or in cones. Animals, water, and the wind spread seeds.

**Deciduous leaves**

Animals and the wind help pollinate a plant when they bring pollen to the parts that make seeds.

Once a seed drops to the ground, it may germinate, or start to grow. The small plant that grows from a seed is called a seedling. The parts of the seed the plant uses as food to begin growing are the seed leaves.

By looking at fossils, scientists can study things that lived long ago. Some fossils are made from extinct plants. These fossils show how plants have changed over time.

**Young tree**

You have read about the basics of how plants and trees grow, live, and change. Now we will dig a little deeper, to get at the roots of tree life.

# Introduction

Trees grow all over the world in many different climates. They are adapted to reproduce and grow in the different environments. Even with these adaptations, all trees have the same basic structure. They all have branches that grow out from a main trunk. The trunk is the stem of the tree. They all have roots that grow from the bottom of the trunk. Roots reach deep into the ground. And all trees have leaves. Some trees have flat leaves. Other trees have leaves shaped like needles.

The kind of bark and roots a tree has also may differ. Some trees have thick bark, while others have thinner bark. Tree roots support trees. They store food made by the tree. They also bring water and minerals to the tree.

**Trees have roots, a trunk, branches, and leaves.**

Leaves

Branch

Trunk

Root

Soil

# Growing Trees

Trees, like most other plants, grow from seeds. Not many seeds grow into mature trees. Some seeds get digested inside animals' bodies after being eaten, and never reach the ground. Other seeds land in places where they cannot grow. If a seed lands in a place with good soil, sunlight, and water, it may start sprouting into a plant. When a seed begins to grow into a plant it is called germination.

## Seed to Sapling

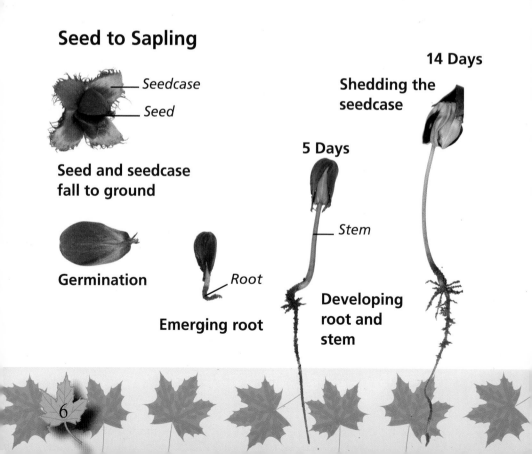

Seedcase
Seed

**Seed and seedcase fall to ground**

**Germination**

**Emerging root**
Root

**5 Days**
Stem

**Developing root and stem**

**14 Days**
**Shedding the seedcase**

First a small root develops. Then a stem begins to grow. After the stem starts growing, the seedcase falls off.

The seed leaves are the plant's first leaves. While the food in these leaves nourishes the plant, the first true leaves form. Those leaves begin to make sugar for the plant to use as food. The seedling may eventually grow into a tree.

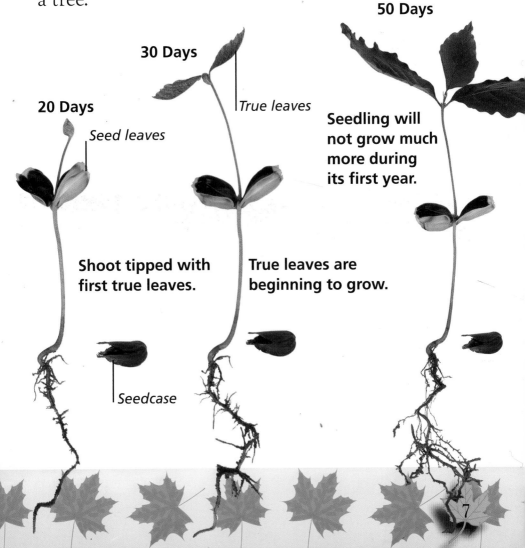

**50 Days**

**30 Days**

*True leaves*

**20 Days**

*Seed leaves*

**Seedling will not grow much more during its first year.**

**Shoot tipped with first true leaves.**

**True leaves are beginning to grow.**

*Seedcase*

# Deciduous Trees

Broadleaf trees have wide, thin leaves. Many broadleaf trees are also deciduous trees. Deciduous trees are adapted to grow in areas with four seasons. They shed their leaves in the fall and grow new leaves each spring. Like all trees, deciduous trees get nutrition through their roots and make food in their leaves.

**A mature oak tree. Oak trees have simple leaves.**

**Oak leaf**

Deciduous trees grow two types of leaves. These are simple leaves and compound leaves. Simple leaves are made up of one leaflet. These leaves are attached to the branches by one main vein. Compound leaves have several leaflets attached to a large stem-like vein. The vein is attached to a branch.

**Elm leaves**

Photosynthesis, the process that green plants use to make food, happens inside chloroplasts. Chloroplasts are special structures in the green parts of leaves that capture energy from sunlight. The leaves use chlorophyll in the chloroplasts to change this energy into sugar, the plant's food.

Deciduous trees are also flowering plants. When the flowers of a deciduous tree have been pollinated, seeds begin to grow inside fruits, nuts, or other seed casings.

**Simple leaf**

**Compound leaf**

When the days become long enough and the air warms in the spring, deciduous trees grow new leaves. Photosynthesis begins in the new leaves. Deciduous trees also blossom with flowers and begin to grow seeds in the spring. Some trees, such as maples, will scatter their seeds in the spring.

In summer there is still plenty of sunlight for photosynthesis. Deciduous trees keep their leaves through the summer. As summer turns to fall, some trees, such as oak and apple trees, scatter their seeds in fruits and nuts.

**Spring**                    **Summer**

The days become shorter as summer turns into fall. The air turns cold. Leaves get their green color from the same chlorophyll that is used in photosynthesis. Once they stop producing chlorophyll, the leaves change from green to red, orange, brown, or yellow. Soon after the leaves turn color, they fall off the trees.

During the winter, the days are short and the air is cold. Deciduous trees shut down many of their systems during the winter. This way they conserve energy during the long, cold winter.

Come spring, leaves begin to grow again. The yearly cycle begins once more.

**Fall** **Winter**

# Coniferous Trees

**Carolina hemlock needles**

Coniferous trees are different from deciduous trees in several important ways. Coniferous leaves are thin and needle shaped. Coniferous leaves are also hard and less flexible, while deciduous leaves are soft and bendable. The leaves of coniferous trees stay on their trees through fall and winter. They are gradually replaced. This is why they are sometimes called evergreen trees.

**The Scotch pine cones open up in order to release their seeds.**

**Mature Scotch pine cone**

**Young Scotch pine cone**

**Coniferous trees keep their leaves in the winter, even when there is a lot of snow.**

Conifers usually grow in areas where the climate is cold. They have one main trunk that grows straight. The branches at the bottom of some coniferous trees are longer and thicker than the branches at the top of the tree. This gives these coniferous trees a conelike shape. The conelike shape helps them drop snow from their branches.

Unlike deciduous trees, conifers do not reproduce with flowers or fruit. Instead, they reproduce using seeds that are held inside cones. The wind helps spread pollen to fertilize the cones. After the seeds in the cone mature, the cone opens and the seeds scatter.

# Tropical Trees

Tropical trees grow in rainforests, or other tropical forests. These forests have layers. The tallest trees of these forests are known as the emergent trees. They stick up above the canopy layer. The canopy layer is just below the emergent trees. Trees that are shorter than the emergent trees make up the canopy. Not much light passes through the canopy layer. The layer of trees below the canopy is known as the midstory layer.

**Different layers of a lowland rainforest in New Zealand**

Tropical trees usually have tall, slender trunks. Their branches, which are long and stretch high into the sky, mostly grow at the top of the tree. Tropical tree branches often get twisted together. Because of this, when one tree falls it may make other trees fall. The gaps created by fallen trees are rapidly filled in by other trees. Tropical trees must grow quickly to get the space and light they need.

**Coconut palm nut**

Some tropical trees reproduce using drift seeds. Drift seeds fall from trees into rivers and oceans. Currents carry them to other areas to sprout. Some tropical trees have special leaves called drip tips. These drip tips are adapted to help rain run off the trees' leaves.

**The drip tips on these leaves are quite pointy.**

# Tree Roots

Trees collect water and minerals through their roots. Roots also anchor trees to the ground. Each root has tiny root hairs that absorb nutrients from the soil and air. Water and minerals are then carried to the rest of the tree.

Root structures are adapted to a tree's environment. For example, fig trees have buttress root structures. Buttress roots grow in tropical climates where the soil is not very good. The main part of the roots grow above the ground. Buttress roots also protect trees against tropical storms by supporting them.

Banyan tree roots, like those of the fig tree, have also adapted to survive in a tropical climate. The roots of a banyan tree grow down from the branches to eventually reach the ground. Banyan trees absorb moisture from the air, rather than the soil, during the first stages of their development.

Roots help anchor the tree to the ground.

The Australian fig's buttress roots grow above the ground.

# Bark and Tree Rings

Tree bark has inner and outer layers. The inner bark carries nutrients up and down the tree. This layer is soft. The outer bark is hard and protects the tree from very hot or very cold temperatures. As trees age, their bark thickens. On some trees the bark may be over one foot thick!

This giant sequoia tree has many rings and thick bark.

**Birch bark is very thin and papery.**

Some tree bark is used to make everyday products. Cork trees have bark that can be used again and again. Rubber tree bark contains a substance that is used to make rubber and latex.

To find out the age of a tree, scientists usually count the number of tree rings it has. Tree rings on very old trees can help scientists determine what the weather was like long ago. In fact, scientists can figure out weather patterns based on tree rings. During wet years trees tend to grow more. That makes their tree rings wider. During dry years the rings are usually thinner.

**Poplar bark is thick and hard.**

# Sowing Seeds

Most plants make seeds to reproduce. Seeds grow after a plant is pollinated. Pollination can happen in several different ways. Some flowering plants produce nectar, a sweet liquid which attracts insects. Butterflies and bees land on the flowers to collect the nectar. Pollen sticks to their bodies and is carried to other flowers.

**Apple blossoms produce fruit after they are pollinated.**

Seeds develop outer coverings for protection. Some seed coverings also help attract animals that scatter seeds. Fruits, berries, and nuts are examples of seed coverings.

Some seeds stick to the fur of animals. That allows animals to carry them to another area to germinate. Other seeds are shaped so that the wind can carry them great distances. They have parts that work like wings to help the seed glide through the air.

**Hawthorn berries can be eaten by people and animals.**

**Maple seeds and horse chestnut seeds have very different seed casings.**

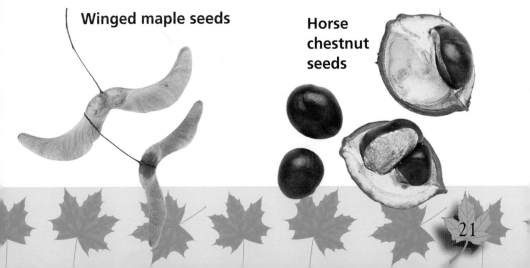

**Winged maple seeds**

**Horse chestnut seeds**

21

# Trees Everywhere

Trees can be found in a variety of shapes. They are adapted to grow in many different climates. Tropical trees grow in warm, wet climates. Coniferous trees grow mainly in cold areas. Deciduous trees do best in places where the weather is very different in winter, spring, summer, and fall. The leaf and root systems of a tree work together to help the tree grow and develop. The roots of a tree bring it water and minerals.

Trees have many everyday uses. The fruit and seeds produced by some trees can be eaten. Tree bark can be used for many household products. Wood from tree trunks and branches is found in almost every home.

Trees have adapted to grow almost everywhere on Earth. They all have certain parts in common. But even with those common parts, each type of tree is different. They have different bark, branches, leaves, roots, and seeds, in order to live where they do.

**Trees in Florida**

# Glossary

**bark**      the tough outside covering of the trunk and branches of trees

**chlorophyll**      the substance in green plants and trees that gives them their color

**compound leaf**      a leaf that is made up of two or more leaflets on a single stalk

**photosynthesis**      the process green plants use to make their own food

**seedcase**      any pod, capsule, or dry, hollow fruit that contains seeds

**simple leaf**      a leaf made up of one leaflet on a single stalk

**tree ring**      the circle in a tree trunk that is added each year as the tree grows thicker

**trunk**      the main stem of a tree